Give Same **COLOR** A Thumbs Up

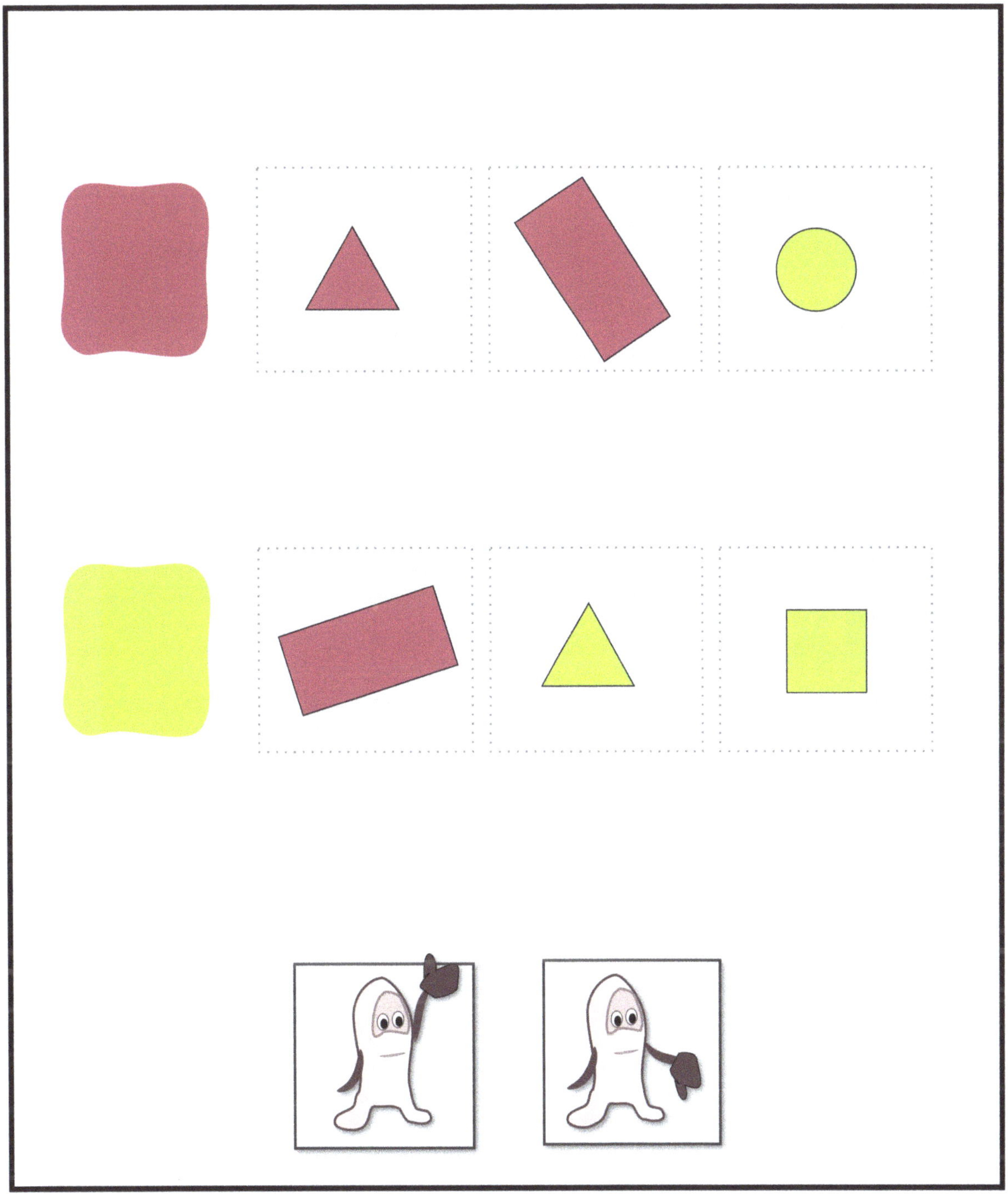

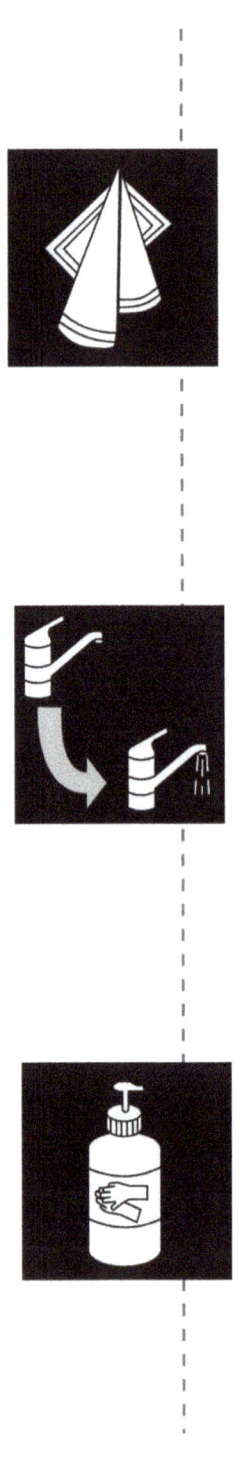

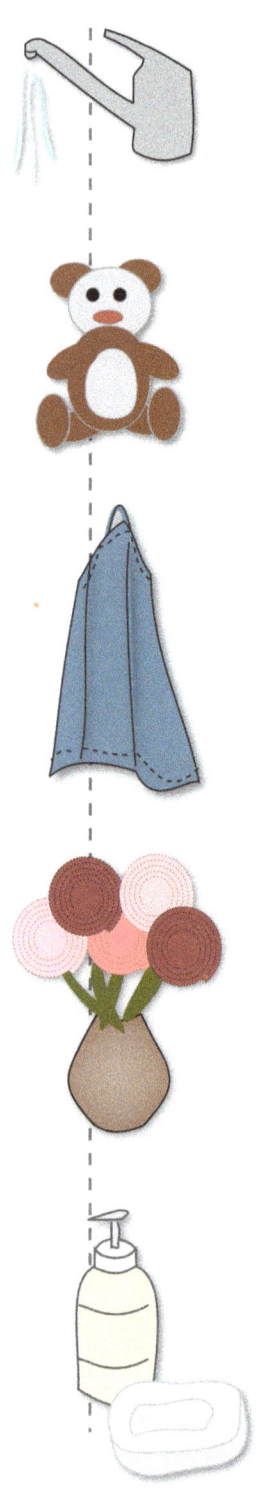

 Find the same! Why do we need it?

Super-A wants to wash hands. Help her turn on water ... wash hands with soap ... dry hands. Give a thumbs up!

Find **ALL**

FIRST   THEN

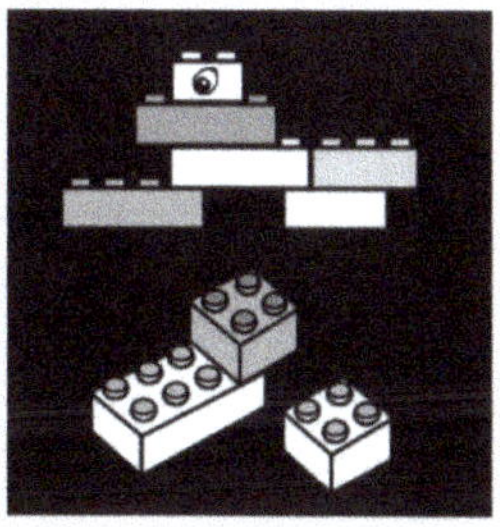

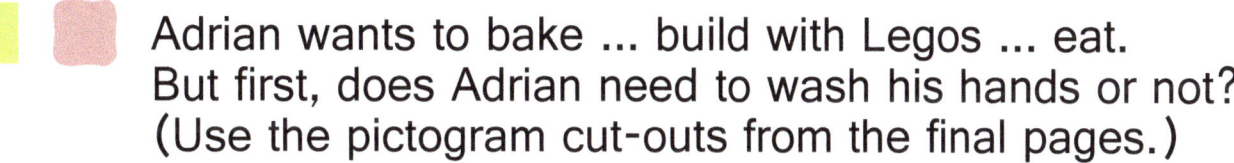

Adrian wants to bake ... build with Legos ... eat.
But first, does Adrian need to wash his hands or not?
(Use the pictogram cut-outs from the final pages.)

FIRST

THEN

 Super-A has used her watercolors ...
Does Super-A need to wash her hands? Why?

FIRST

THEN

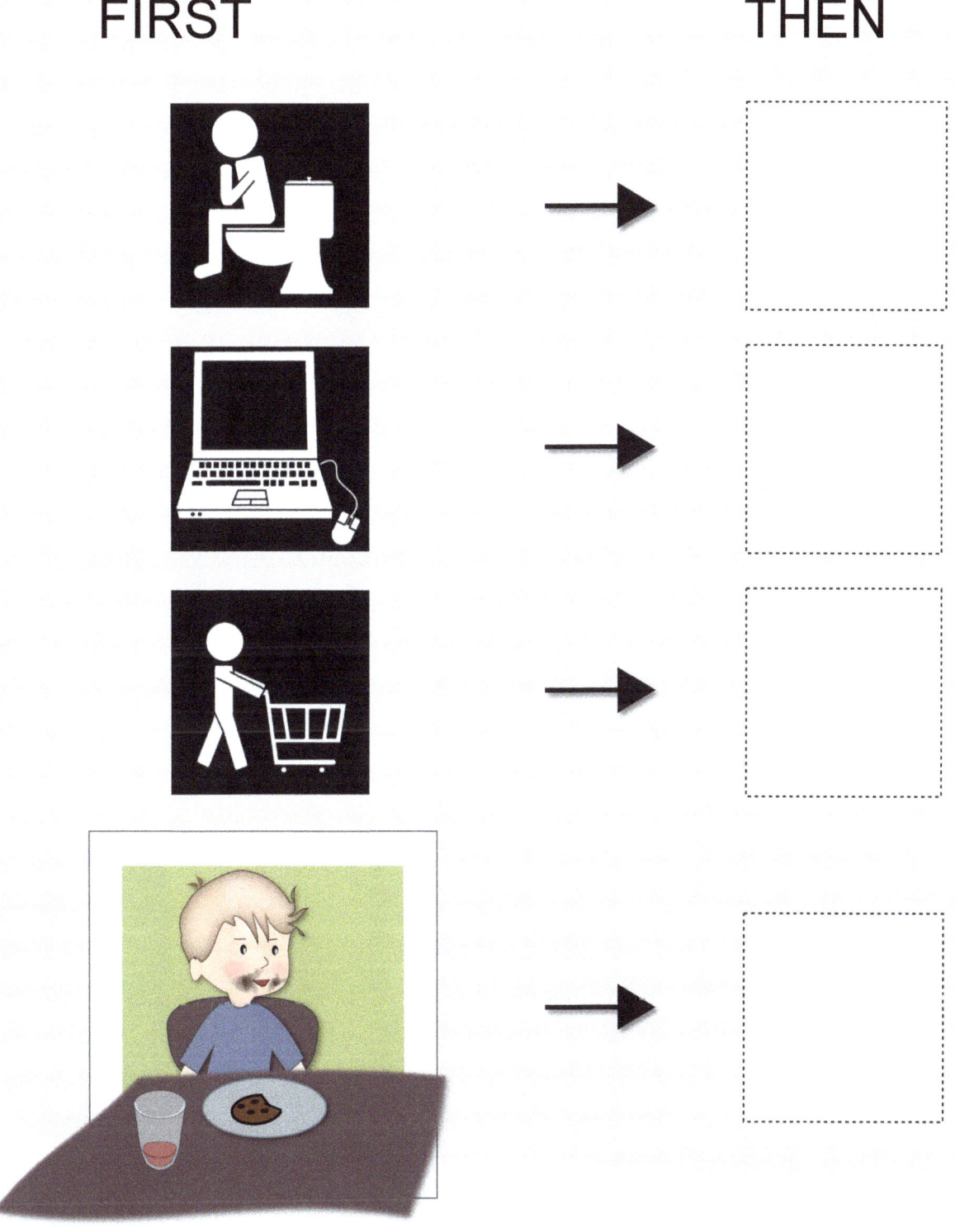

Adrian has used the toilet ...
Does Adrian need to wash his hands? Why?

Find **ALL**

Everybody wants to wash hands!
Help them wait their turn. Who gets soap first?
(Cut out the person cards from the final pages.)

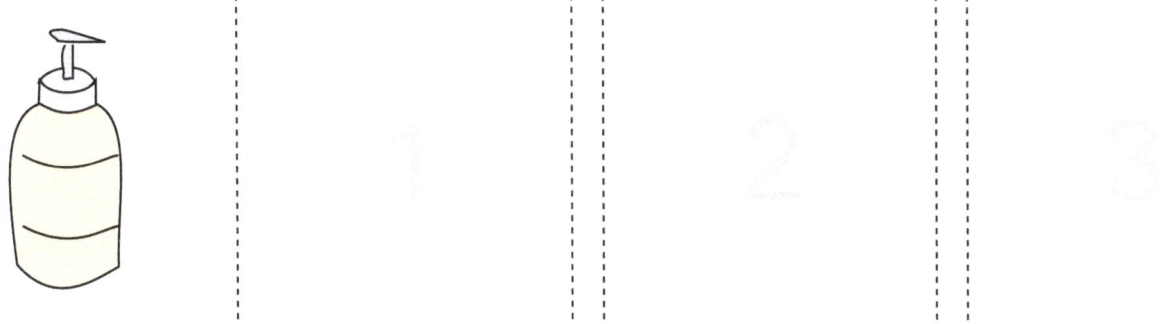

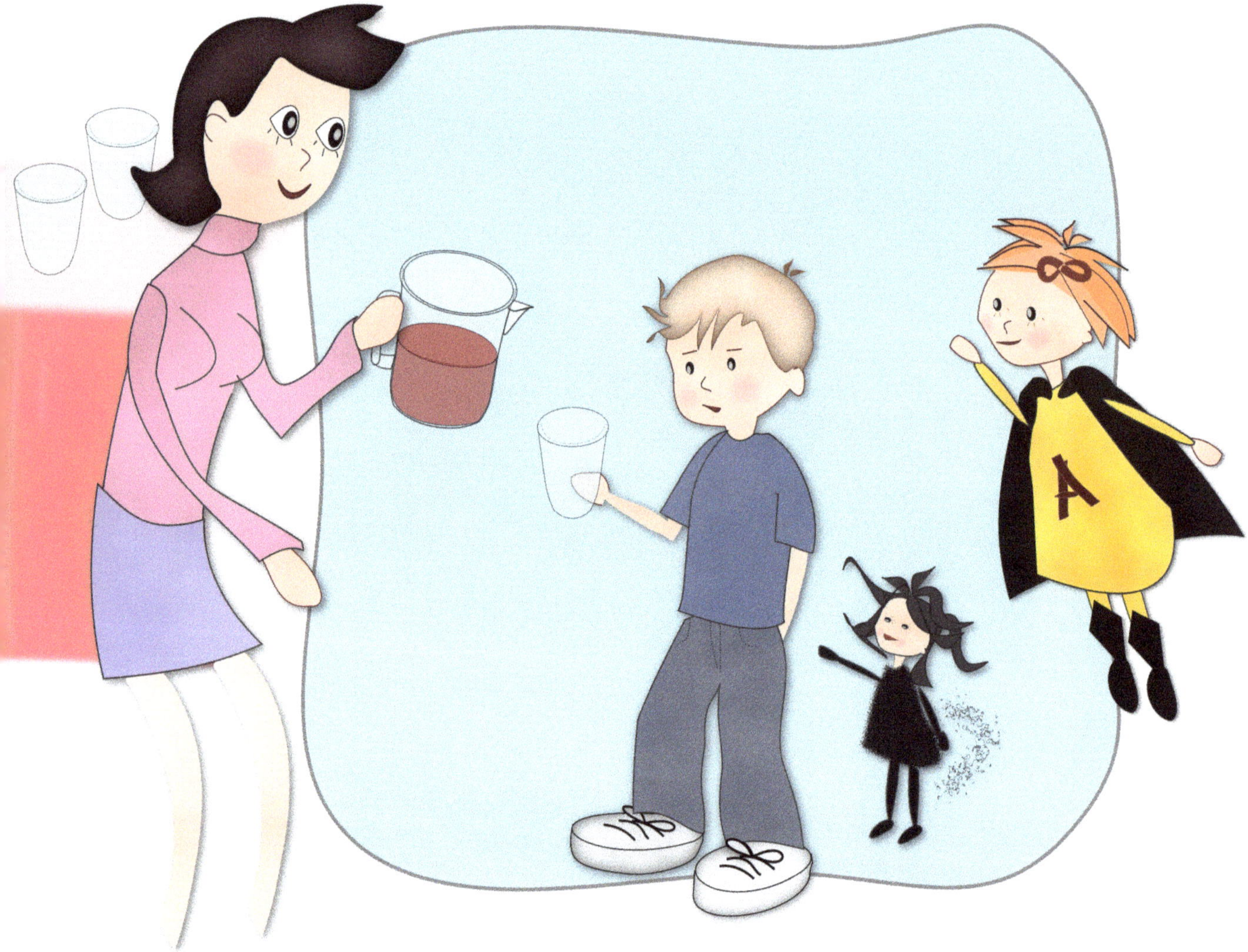

Everybody wants to drink!
Help them wait their turn. Who gets to drink first?

1	2	3

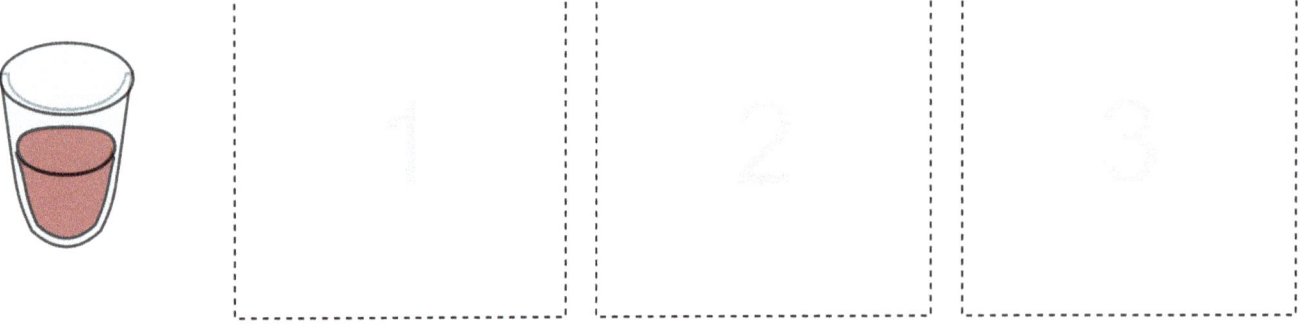

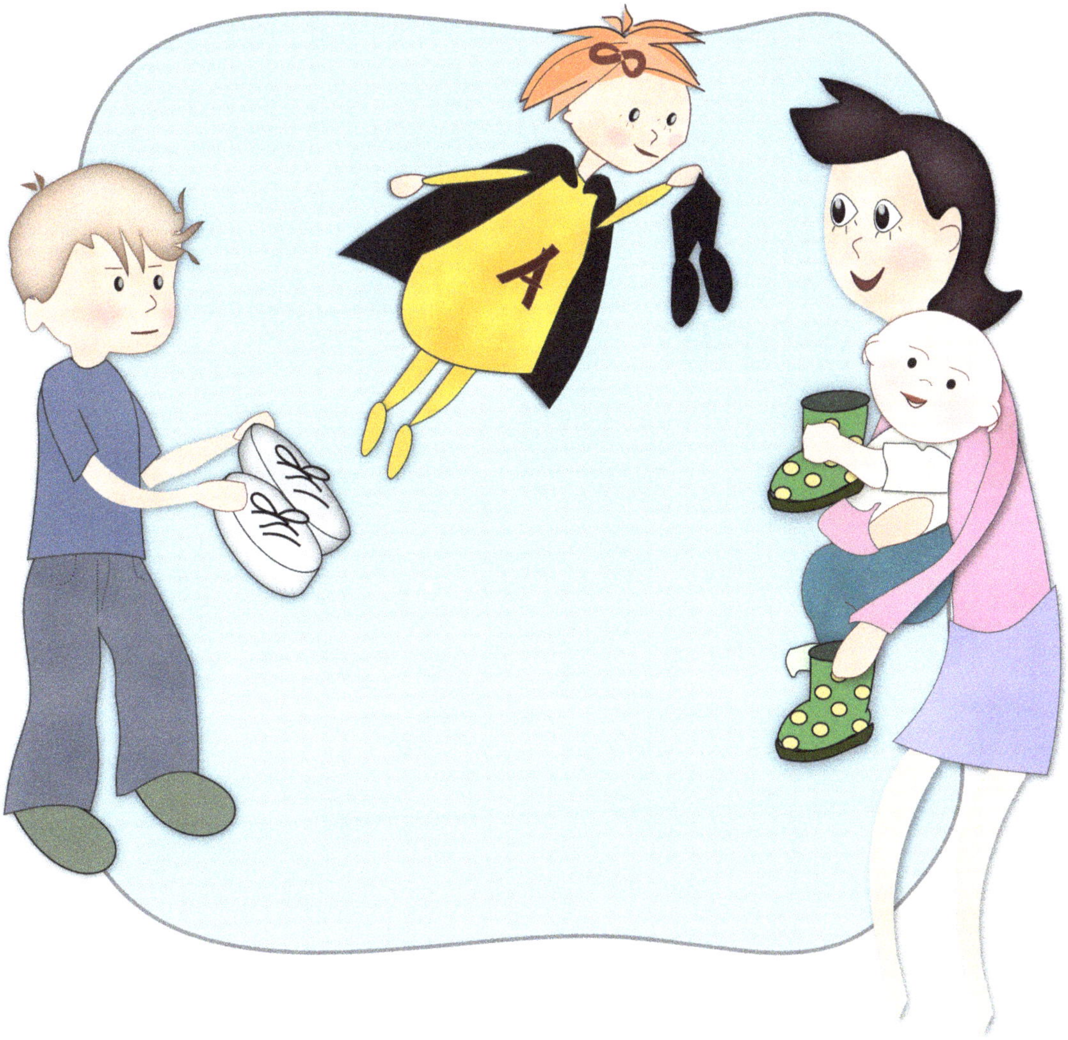

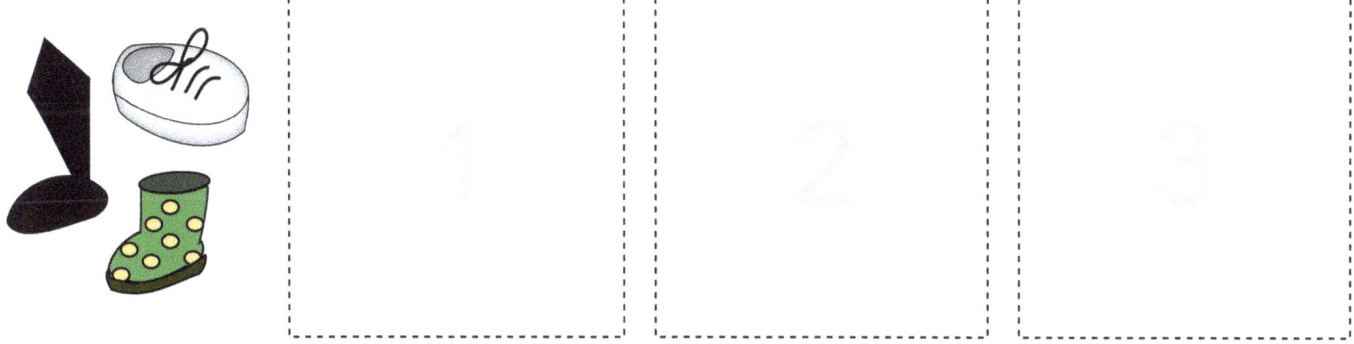

Everybody wants Mom to help with their shoes!
Help them wait their turn. Who gets to put on shoes first?

1 2 3

Super-A wants to wash her hands.
What does not belong? Give a thumbs down!

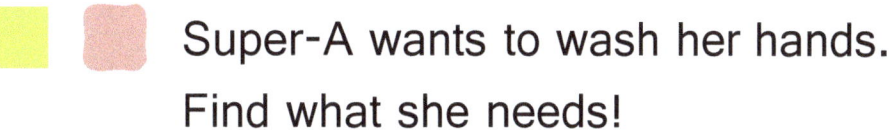

Super-A wants to wash her hands.
Find what she needs!

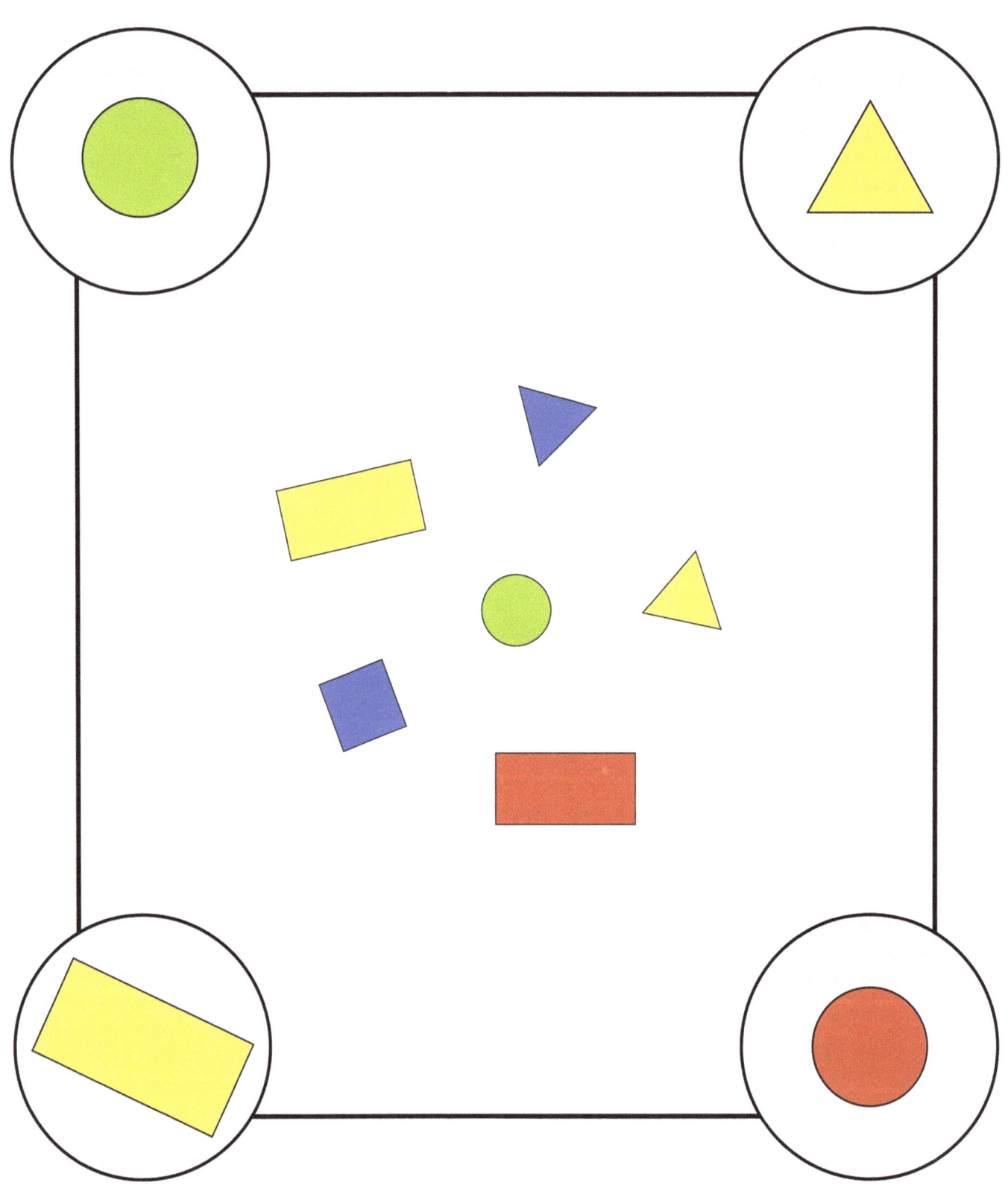

Find **?** Same

Wait! Adrian and Super-A cannot have a snack yet.
What should Mom bring to the table first?

 OR

 Wait! Who should do it? Why?
Give a thumbs up ... or down.

OR

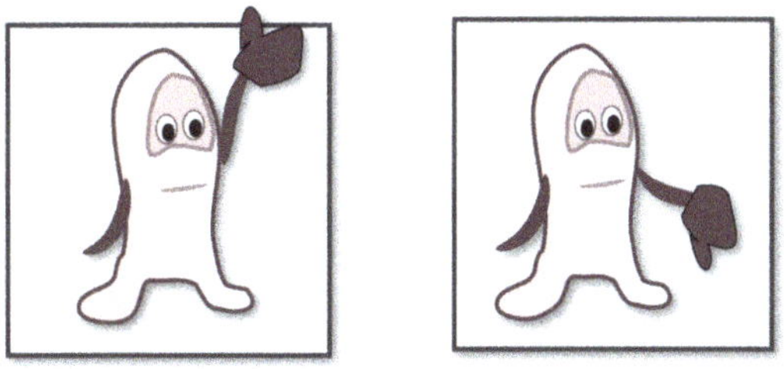

OR

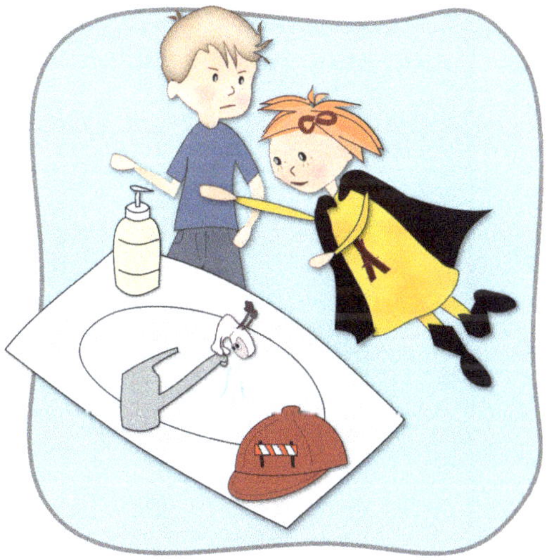

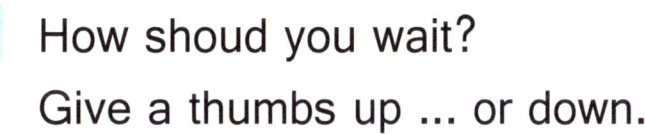

How shoud you wait?
Give a thumbs up ... or down.

Find **4 BLOCKS** To Build

THUMBS UP

THUMBS DOWN

We ... dry our hands ... wash our hands ... take soap ... mix ... and bake. What is right?

(Cut out the memory cards. Play memory and give a thumbs up or down for each pair.)

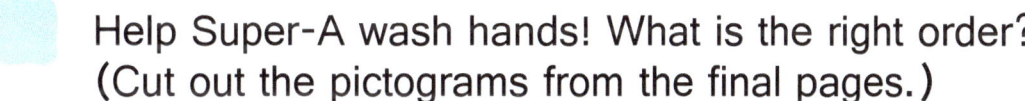

Help Super-A wash hands! What is the right order?
(Cut out the pictograms from the final pages.)

1	2	3	4	5

Dad goes to get the bottle. Who waits for it?
Place the red Wait-cap on Adrian, the baby or Mom.
(Cut out the circles and the cap on the next page.)

Cut-outs for the exercises. Above: Wash hands before/after.
Below: Help them wait their turn. Order the pictograms.

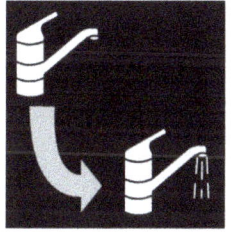    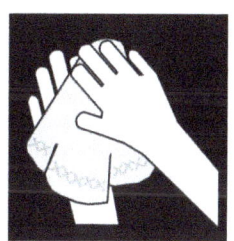

  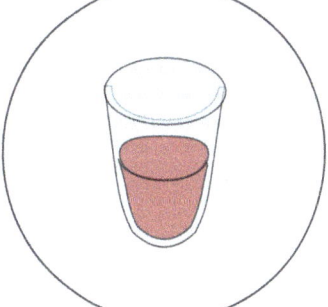 

Add your own photos to the circles and teach your child to wait for things.

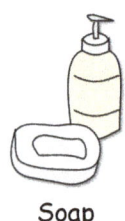
Soap

Oven Mitt

Butter

Eggs

Do you want to get to know Adrian and Super-A better?
There are more workbooks and books!

Be My Rails Publishing

www.BeMyRails.com

| Open Tap | Take Soap | Wash with Soap | Close Tap | Take Towel | Dry Hands |

Use the pictograms with Raily the Train!
(From the STARTERS Workbook 1)

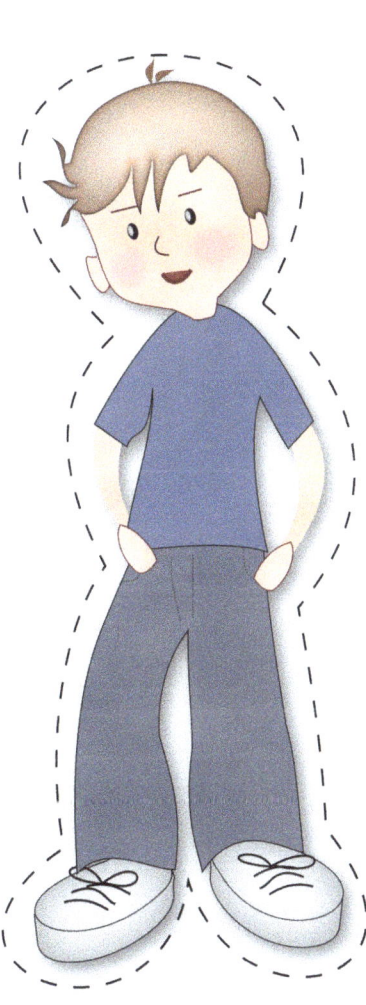

Our friends from the Adrian and Super-A books and workbooks!